The CENTER SOLUTION

Ideas For Classroom Learning Centers

Written by Linda Schwartz
Illustrated by Bev Armstrong

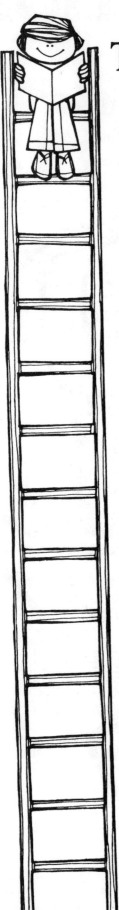

THE LEARNING WORKS

P.O. Box 6187 Santa Barbara, CA 93160

The purchase of this book entitles the
individual teacher to reproduce copies for use
in the classroom.

The reproduction of any part for an entire
school or school system or for commercial
use is strictly prohibited.

No form of this work may be reproduced
or transmitted or recorded without written
permission from the publisher.

INTRODUCTION

THE CENTER SOLUTION was designed for the classroom teacher in search of stimulating ideas, projects, and activities for use at learning centers. The activities presented help promote independent, self-directed learning and allow students to make individual choices and decisions. The flexible format of THE CENTER SOLUTION allows the teacher to write specific objectives for each center according to students' grade levels and abilities. Many of the ideas can be extended and applied to other subject areas.

Each activity consists of a concise summary for the teacher, a list of materials and supplies needed, and instructions for the students. The "More Ideas" section in many activities provides suggestions for additional reinforcement of the concepts presented. The activities in this book may be carried out by students working directly at learning centers, or the centers can be set up with materials and supplies for students to use at their seats.

THE CENTER SOLUTION is divided into three main sections:

RESEARCH SKILL CENTERS: Activities in this section are project-oriented and involve students in long-range research. A sketch is drawn to suggest various ways each center may be displayed. The student directions, written in easily understandable terms, may be placed directly at the center, or teachers may prefer to make a ditto for each student. Students can pursue individual interests while working around a common core. Many of the projects lend themselves to small group participation.

CREATIVE WRITING SKILL CENTERS: The activities in this section are aimed at giving students an opportunity to really stretch their imaginations. Projects include writing poetry, demonstrating creative thinking, and examining values and self-concepts. The directions for the students include an illustration of a sample completed project.

DICTIONARY SKILL CENTERS: This section helps to develop and reinforce research skills such as alphabetizing, use of guide words, pronunciation, and finding word context clues. Creative ideas make the dictionary a "fun" tool for learning and research. Worksheets are provided for each activity and may be reproduced for each student in the class.

CONTENTS

RESEARCH CENTERS

FIVE FALSE FACTS CENTER

A CENTER SUMMARY

Students decorate a shoebox on a specific theme. After doing research on the topic, students write fifteen true facts and five false facts about the topic chosen. Students mix and number all twenty cards and place them in the box. Classmates try to guess the FIVE FALSE FACTS after reading all the cards. Completed boxes make an excellent bulletin board display. *(See diagram below.)*

MATERIALS NEEDED

shoebox
lined 3 x 5 index cards (21 per pupil)
encyclopedias and reference materials
pencils or pens
colored paper to decorate shoebox
crayons, magic markers
scissors
glue
envelopes (1 per pupil for the numbers of the five wrong facts)

For suggested topics, see page 16.

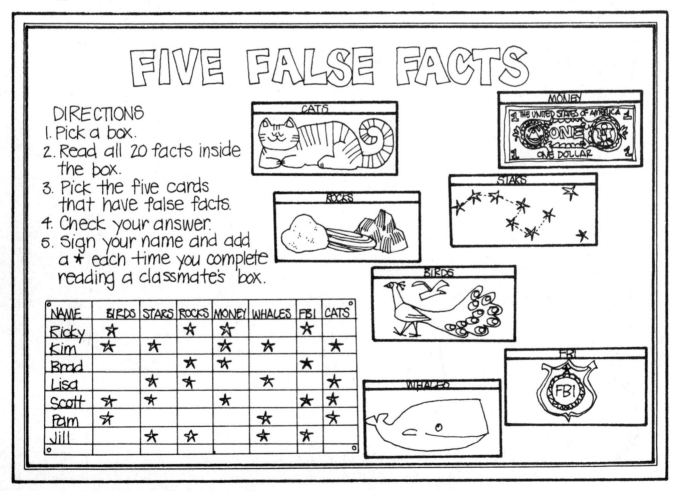

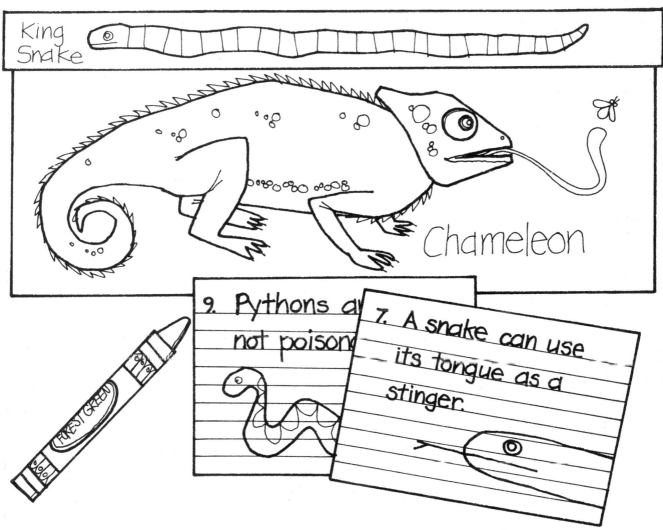

1. Pick a subject you would like to learn more about.

2. Decorate a shoebox on the theme of your topic. Decorate all the sides as well as the top of the box. Print the title of your study on the top of your box.

3. Research your topic and take notes.

4. Using your notes, write fifteen interesting facts on index cards — only one fact per card.

5. Now make up five false facts about your topic, and write these on index cards, one per card.

6. Mix all twenty cards together and number each card.

7. Place all twenty cards in your decorated box. Write the numbers of the five false facts on a card, and place the card in an envelope inside the box.

8. See if your classmates can guess your FIVE FALSE FACTS.

ALL ABOUT AN ANIMAL CENTER

A CENTER SUMMARY

Students select an animal for an in-depth study. After doing research and taking notes, students are given four choices of follow-up activities involving writing and art skills.

MATERIALS NEEDED

encyclopedias and reference books on animals
colored paper
white drawing paper
pencils or pens
crayons, magic markers
scissors
glue
rulers
wire coat hanger and thread (project B)
shoebox (project C)

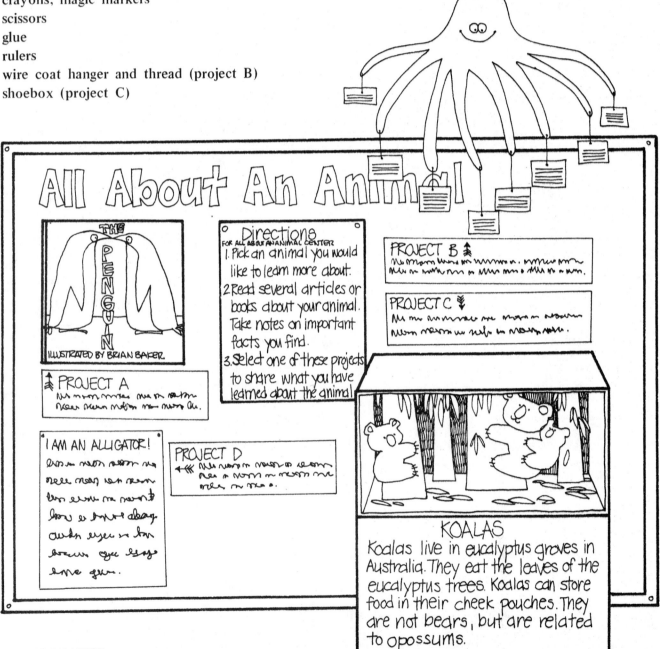

DIRECTIONS FOR
ALL ABOUT AN ANIMAL CENTER

1. Pick an animal you would like to learn more about.

2. Read several articles or books about your animal. Takes notes on important facts you find.

3. Select one of the following projects to share what you have learned about the animal:

PROJECT A

An author has written a book about the animal you studied and wants YOU to illustrate a book cover. You are also hired to write a summary for the inside jacket telling what the book is about.

PROJECT B

The local zoo has hired you to design a mobile about the animal you selected that will provide factual information. It must also be colorful and attractive so it will sell well in the zoo gift shop.

PROJECT C

The museum in town has asked you to make a diorama showing your animal in its natural habitat. (Your diorama should be done in a box suitable for display.)

PROJECT D

A popular children's magazine has assigned the following story to you: Pretend you ARE the animal you studied. Write a story about your life telling what you eat, where you can be found, who your enemies are, what your habits are, how you help or hinder man, how you protect your-self, your characteristics such as size and weight, unusual things, etc.

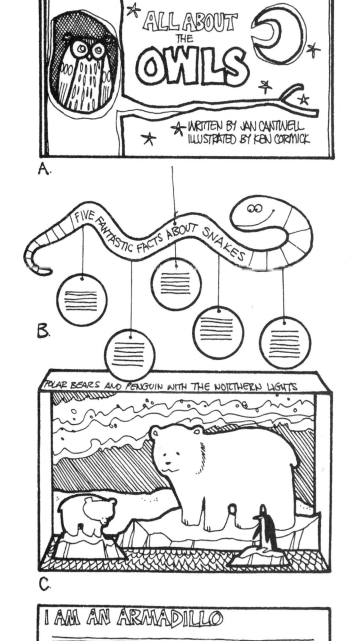

A.

B.

C.

D.

COMMUNICATION CUBE CENTER

A CENTER SUMMARY

Students select a form of communication to study. After doing research and taking notes, students cover a carton with colored construction paper and fill all sides with data and pictures of their form of communication. The completed COMMUNICATION CUBES can then be stacked or hung from the ceiling as mobiles.

MATERIALS NEEDED

encyclopedias and reference materials on communication
small cardboard cartons
colored construction paper
tape
scissors
glue
magazines (for pictures)
pens
colored pencils, magic markers, crayons

SUGGESTED TOPICS FOR COMMUNICATION

braille	Morse code	printing
television	codes	advertising
radio	sports signals	hieroglyphics
flags	lights and bells	picture symbols
lasers	animal communication	books
sign language	newspapers	movies

CENTER SOLUTION

1. Pick a form of communication you would like to study and learn more about.

2. Read about your type of communication in encyclopedias and reference books.

3. Take notes on interesting facts you learn.

4. Cover a grocery box with colored paper.

5. Write the topic you selected in large letters on one side of the box.

6. Decorate and fill all sides of your box with important facts you have learned.
   Add lots of pictures and illustrations.

7. Display your COMMUNICATION CUBE for others to share.

EDUCATIONAL GAME CENTER

A CENTER SUMMARY

Students create an educational game that other students can play. This is an ideal project for small groups. Students make up question cards, design a playing board, make tokens, devise rules and directions, and decorate a box for the game contents.

MATERIALS NEEDED

scratch paper (for rough draft)
white posterboard for final playing board
encyclopedias and reference materials for research
magic markers, pencils
rulers
scissors
colored art paper for question cards (2" x 4")
glue (for attaching rules to inside box cover)
dice or spinner
tokens for up to 4 players
boxes for game contents (such as dress boxes)

TO MAKE A SPINNER, CUT A SHAPE LIKE THIS FROM LIGHT CARDBOARD. INSERT A SHORT PENCIL OR SHARPENED DOWEL THROUGH CENTER. SPIN LIKE A TOP; NUMBER TOUCHING GROUND WHEN SPINNER STOPS IS THE NUMBER YOU HAVE "ROLLED"

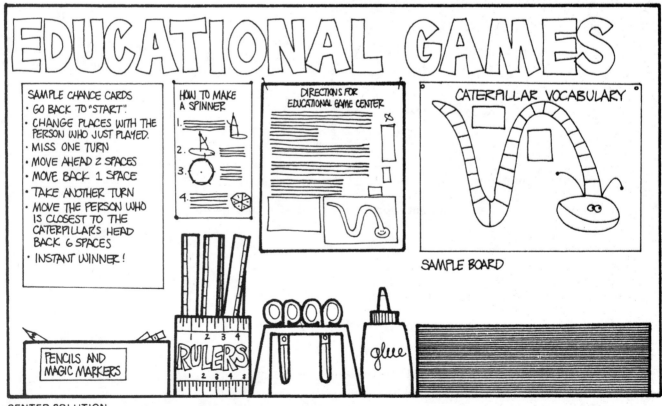

CENTER SOLUTION

DIRECTIONS FOR
EDUCATIONAL GAME CENTER

1. Pick a partner to work with. Make an educational game for 2-4 players.

2. Pick a subject for your game or combine any two of the following:

   science, history, spelling, math, vocabulary, grammar, famous people, etc.

3. Your game should include:
   a. an original name
   b. grade level for players (example: grades 4-6)
   c. object or purpose of game
   d. a theme to go with the subject of your game such as "Fraction Fun"
   e. dice or spinner
   f. playing pieces for 2-4 players
   g. question cards
   h. chance cards
   i. answer booklet
   j. rules and directions for play
   k. playing board
   l. box for game contents

4. Design a rough draft of your game. Make sure the name of your game is clear and easy to read.

5. Make up about 30 question cards using reference books. Also add some chance cards to make your game interesting such as "out of gas, lose a turn."

6. Copy the rough draft on white posterboard. Use a ruler and work neatly. Add pictures to make your board attractive and fun. Color your board.

7. Make tokens for four players.

8. Design a box for your game equipment such as dice, question and chance cards, play money, spinners, etc. (Your board does not have to fit inside the box.)

9. Paste your rules and directions inside the box cover. Your rules should answer the following questions:
   a. What is the object of the game?
   b. Who goes first?
   c. What do you do when you land on a square?
   d. Who checks the answers in the answer booklet?
   e. What happens if you answer a question correctly? Incorrectly?
   f. When is the game over?

SPINNER

SAMPLE ANSWER BOOK

CATERPILLAR VOCABULARY ANSWERS
1. SEPIA IS BROWN
2. KIWIS ARE BIRDS
3. LICHEN IS A PLANT
4. BUFFOON IS A CLOWN
5. AUK IS A BIRD
6. MANGO IS A FRUIT
7. GOURAMI IS A FISH
8. OKRA IS A VEGETABLE
9. MUSLIN IS CLOTH
10. PAPAYA IS A FRUIT

SAMPLE CHANCE CARD

GO AHEAD 2 SPACES.

SAMPLE QUESTION CARD

IS A KIWI A FISH, A BIRD, OR A MAMMAL? ②

Rules
1. Spin the spinner to see how many spaces you can move.
2. If you land on a "C", take a chance card. If you land on a "?", take a question card.
3. If you cannot answer the question, you must go back to "START". If you can, stay where you are until your next turn.

CENTER SOLUTION

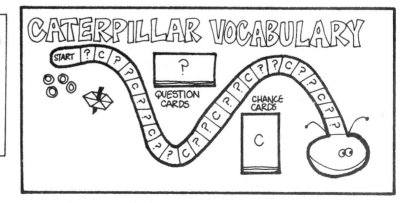

CREATE-A-KIT CENTER

A CENTER SUMMARY

At the Create-a-Kit Center, students do research on a specific topic and then make a study kit for another student to use. This individualized study kit contains data, test questions, follow-up activities, illustrations, evaluations, etc. (Suggested topics and a sample evaluation sheet are on pages 16 and 17.)

MATERIALS NEEDED

file folders (for kit contents)
writing paper for data
white art paper for illustrations and pictures
encyclopedias and other reference materials
scissors
pencils and pens
magazines (for pictures)
glue

CENTER SOLUTION

You are going to make an individualized study kit for another student to use.

1. Pick a subject that you would like to learn more about.

2. Decorate a file folder to go with your topic. Your name and the title of your kit should go on the outside. Put all the contents inside as you work.

3. Your completed kit should contain the following:
   a. a title page
   b. a table of contents to tell where to find things in the kit
   c. approximately three pages of information about the topic you chose
   d. ten or more test questions about the information so other students using your kit can see how much they learned (Be sure to make an answer sheet so students can check their test.)
   e. pictures, illustrations, maps — whatever fits best with the topic you chose
   f. a follow-up puzzle, maze or activity related to your topic
   g. an evaluation of the kit for students to complete (This will tell you how much they enjoyed your kit and what suggestions they have for changes.)

4. When your kit is complete, share it with your classmates so they can learn more about the topic you chose.

SUGGESTED TOPICS for CREATE-A-KIT

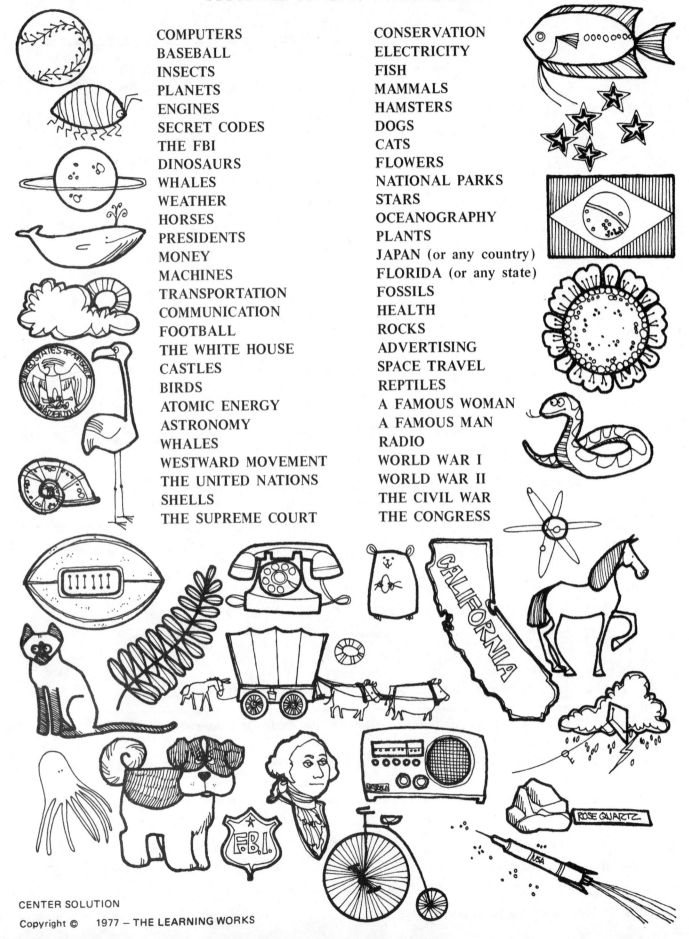

COMPUTERS	CONSERVATION
BASEBALL	ELECTRICITY
INSECTS	FISH
PLANETS	MAMMALS
ENGINES	HAMSTERS
SECRET CODES	DOGS
THE FBI	CATS
DINOSAURS	FLOWERS
WHALES	NATIONAL PARKS
WEATHER	STARS
HORSES	OCEANOGRAPHY
PRESIDENTS	PLANTS
MONEY	JAPAN (or any country)
MACHINES	FLORIDA (or any state)
TRANSPORTATION	FOSSILS
COMMUNICATION	HEALTH
FOOTBALL	ROCKS
THE WHITE HOUSE	ADVERTISING
CASTLES	SPACE TRAVEL
BIRDS	REPTILES
ATOMIC ENERGY	A FAMOUS WOMAN
ASTRONOMY	A FAMOUS MAN
WHALES	RADIO
WESTWARD MOVEMENT	WORLD WAR I
THE UNITED NATIONS	WORLD WAR II
SHELLS	THE CIVIL WAR
THE SUPREME COURT	THE CONGRESS

SAMPLE EVALUATION SHEET FOR   CREATE-A-KIT
(To be used by the student who uses your kit)

Student's name _____ Grade _____
using the kit   level

1. I just completed the kit called _____.

2. This kit was written by _____.

3. I thought this kit was   a) excellent   b) very good   c) fair   d) poor

4. The information pages taught me:

   a) many new facts   b) some new facts   c) no new facts

5. This kit was: a) too easy for me   b) too hard for me   c) just right for me

6. Score each of the following: ☆ excellent   √ good   – fair

   _____ cover of kit   _____ information   _____ test questions

   _____ pictures   _____ puzzles   _____ handwriting

7. The part of the kit I liked best was _____.

8. The part of the kit I liked least was _____.

THESE ARE JUST SUGGESTIONS – MAKE UP SOME OF YOUR OWN
EVALUATION QUESTIONS.

BROCHURES FOR TOURS CENTER

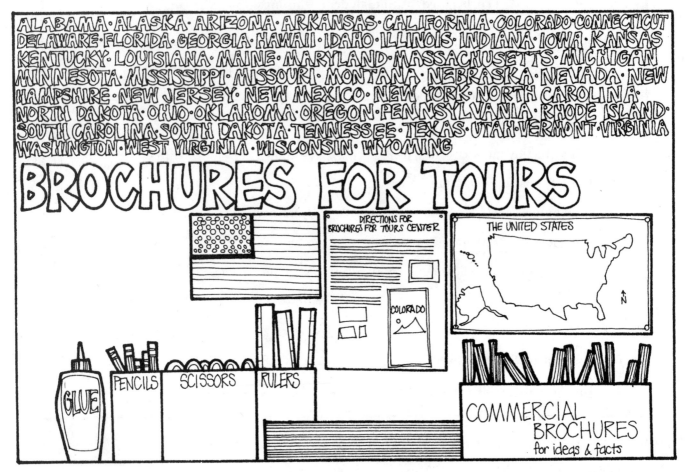

A CENTER SUMMARY

Students select a state they are interested in learning more about. After doing research on the state, students design a travel brochure using suggested topics as a guide for research.

MATERIALS NEEDED

encyclopedias and reference materials on states
scratch paper for planning
white art paper for brochure
magic markers
rulers
pencils and pens
magazines (for pictures)
scissors
glue
*Travel agencies are an excellent source for pamphlets, maps, and pictures.

MORE IDEAS . . .

Instead of making a folded brochure, the same ideas can be used on posterboard divided into sections. Each section is filled with facts or pictures about the state.

CENTER SOLUTION

DIRECTIONS FOR
BROCHURES FOR TOURS CENTER

1. Select a state you would like to learn more about. Write to the State Chamber of Commerce for free information. Be sure to include your home address.

2. Read about this state. Take notes on important facts you find.

3. Make a travel brochure for the state you selected. Make your brochure attractive and informative so classmates will want to visit this state.

4. Include the following information:
   a. name of the state you selected
   b. map of the state
   c. important features such as mountains or rivers
   d. five important cities in your state
   e. interesting places to visit
   f. sports and recreation
   g. important industries
   h. historical landmarks
   i. history and famous people of this state
   j. other interesting facts you discovered

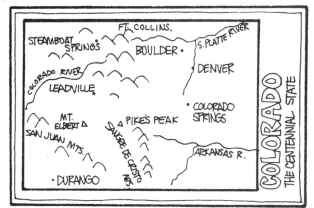

5. Fold your paper as shown below. Fill each section of your brochure with pictures and facts about the state you selected.

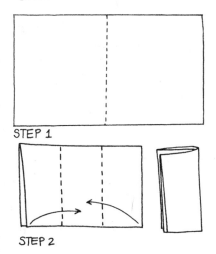

STEP 1

STEP 2

PEOPLE IN PROFILE CENTER

A CENTER SUMMARY

Students select a famous woman or man in any of the following fields: politics, entertainment, sports, medicine, science, education, etc. After doing research and taking notes, students write reports and draw a portrait of their person. (The reports are written in first person as if the student were actually the person chosen.) Each student contributes one page to a class People in Profile booklet. The entire booklet can then be assembled and displayed in the classroom with a cover entitled: PEOPLE IN PROFILE.

MATERIALS NEEDED

encyclopedias, reference books, and biographies of famous people
paper and pencils for notes
white art paper for portrait
notebook paper for final copy of report
colored paper for mounting report and picture
magic markers for illustrations
pens
glue

MORE IDEAS . . .

1. After completing their reports, students can dress as their person and give oral reports to the class — a great way to share new facts learned.

2. The class can pretend they are news reporters and then interview each "famous person" by asking questions about his or her life.

THEODOR SEUSS GEISEL

THE CAT IN THE HAT

FROM A DRAWING BY DR. SEUSS

My name is Theodor Seuss Geisel, but you probably know me by my pen name, which is "Dr. Seuss". I have written and illustrated a lot of books for children. Some of them are <u>Horton Hears a Who</u>, <u>How the Grinch Stole Christmas</u>, <u>The Cat in the Hat</u>, and <u>Bartholomew and the Oobleck</u>.

I love to imagine things. If you have read some of my stories, you know that they are full of imaginary plants and animals, and even imaginary words!

I live in La Jolla, California, on a hill near the ocean. From my house I can see whales going by, fog coming in from the ocean, and even the mountains of Mexico. I think it helps my imagination to be able to

1. Pick a famous man or woman you would like to learn more about. Here are a few suggestions to give you an idea:

Florence Nightingale	Booker T. Washington
Babe Ruth	Amelia Earhart
Betsy Ross	Pablo Picasso
John F. Kennedy	Dorothy Hammill
Helen Keller	Louisa May Alcott
Martin Luther King	Eleanor Roosevelt
Marian Anderson	Ludwig van Beethoven
Albert Einstein	Thomas Jefferson

2. Read about your person and take notes about important facts you learn.

3. Write a report about two pages long. Write as if you *were* the person you selected. For example: My name is Amelia Earhart. I was born in the little town of _____ in the year _____ . I first became interested in flying when . . . .

4. Draw a picture of your person or a scene showing something important that happened in your person's life.

5. Paste the report on one side of a large sheet of colored paper. Paste the picture on the other side. Write your person's name in large letters across the top of the colored paper as shown in the example.

STAMP SCAVENGER HUNT CENTER

A CENTER SUMMARY

Each student picks a stamp of a country at the STAMP SCAVENGER HUNT CENTER.
The stamp is used as a basis for research to answer specific questions about the country.
Findings are recorded in a student notebook.

MATERIALS NEEDED

stamps of countries (cut out the stamps on pages 23 and 24 and have each student
  pick a stamp at the center)
encyclopedias and reference materials
travel folders (get from travel agencies)
writing paper
pencils and pens
ditto of scavenger hunt questions
colored construction paper (for cover)
crayons, magic markers
scissors
glue
magazines (for pictures and articles on countries)
stapler (for binding notebook)

CENTER SOLUTION

SWEDEN

HAULING CORK BARK

PORTUGAL

DENMARK

BLARNEY CASTLE

IRELAND

SPAIN

SWITZERLAND

FINLAND

BELGIUM

GREECE

ISRAEL

ICELAND

GERMANY

INDIA

AUSTRIA

ITALY

POLAND

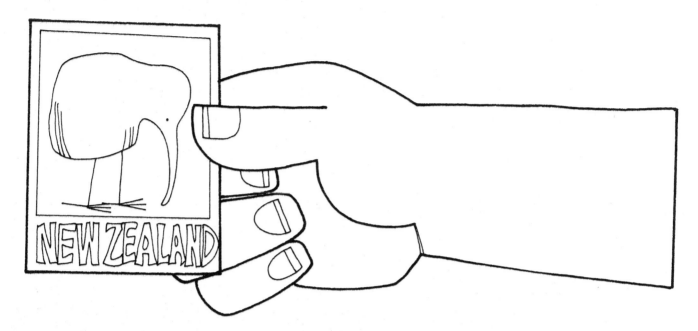

1. Pick a stamp of a country from the center. This is YOUR country to investigate.

2. Make a notebook about your country. Using encyclopedias, magazines, and other reference materials, find the answers to these SCAVENGER HUNT questions:

   a. What are the names and locations of three important cities in this country?

   b. What are some favorite foods of this country? Describe them.

   c. What is the weather like in this country?

   d. What type of government does this country have? How does it differ from the country you live in?

   e. Describe the transportation used in this country.

   f. Name and describe three types of sports or recreation people of this country enjoy.

   g. How is the education of this country different from or similar to that in the country you live in?

   h. How do the people dress in this country? Make an illustration.

   i. List and describe three places of interest a tourist should visit.

   j. What does this country look like? Draw a map and include cities, mountains, lakes, rivers, etc.

   k. How do the houses and buildings differ from those you are familiar with?

   l. What is the name of an important leader of this country today?

When all your facts have been gathered, bind them in a notebook. Decorate the cover with an enlarged picture of your stamp or design your own. Also fill your notebook with illustrations, pictures of the country, charts, and newspaper articles about this country today.

CENTER SOLUTION

A PROBLEM POSTER CENTER

A CENTER SUMMARY

Students select a special theme for investigation and research based on a current problem such as water pollution, crime, or endangered species. Using facts and pictures from magazines and newspapers, students make a PROBLEM POSTER on their topic. Illustrations, editorials, headlines, letters to the editor, magazine pictures, and newspaper articles all become a part of the poster.

MATERIALS NEEDED

magazines
newspapers
encyclopedias and other reference materials
posterboard
scissors
glue

MORE IDEAS . . .

Have students express their feeling and opinions on their topics by writing "Letters to the Editor" and submitting them to a local newspaper.

OR

Have students organize a panel discussion on the problems the class selected.

CENTER SOLUTION

DIRECTIONS FOR
A PROBLEM POSTER CENTER

1. Pick a problem of special interest to you such as:

   a. water pollution

   b. air pollution

   c. poverty

   d. noise pollution

   e. crime

   f. endangered species

   g. drugs

   h. energy shortages

   i. water conservation

   j. inflation

   k. unemployment

2. Collect and cut out headlines, articles, editorials, pictures, and information about this topic from magazines and newspapers.

3. Make a PROBLEM POSTER about your topic. Glue your articles and pictures on a piece of posterboard.

4. Display your PROBLEM POSTER for others to share.

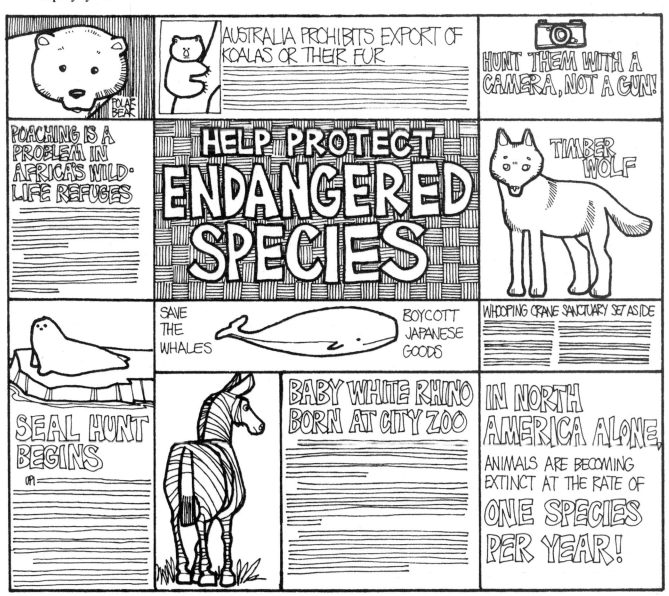

NOTES

CREATIVE WRITING CENTERS

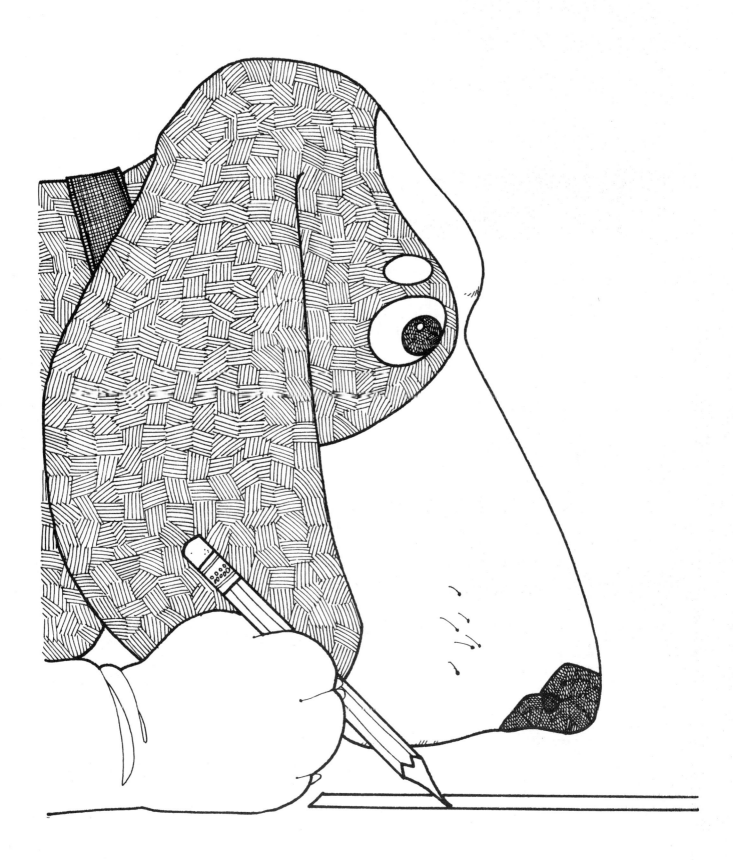

PERSONALITY CUBE CENTER

A CENTER SUMMARY

Students cover a cardboard box with pictures, sketches, and slogans cut from magazines that tell about their likes, dislikes, personality, plans for the future and general life style.

MATERIALS NEEDED

cardboard box
scissors
glue
magazines (for pictures and slogans)
magic markers
colored paper

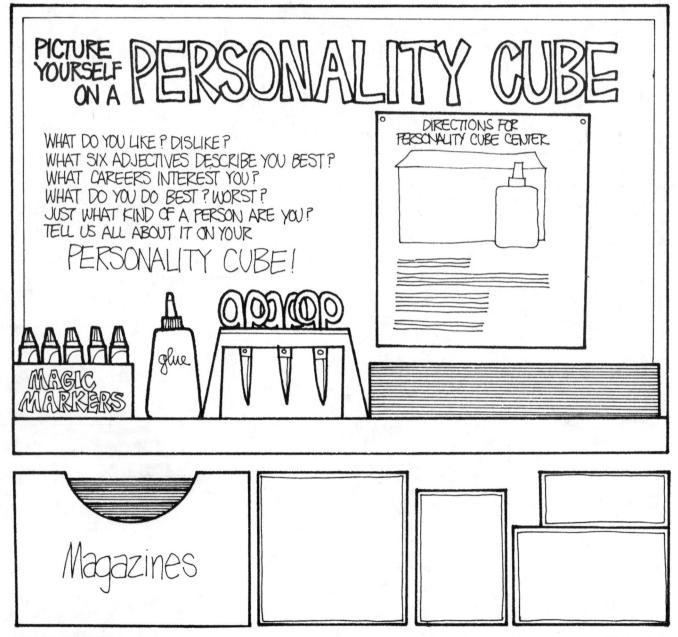

CENTER SOLUTION

1. Bring a cardboard box to class.

2. Cover the box with colored paper.

3. Decorate the box with pictures and slogans from magazines or draw your own sketches that tell about your:

   a. likes
   b. dislikes
   c. personality
   d. hobbies and interests
   e. strengths and weaknesses
   f. plans for the future

THE GLOVE CENTER

A CENTER SUMMARY

Students pick a glove from several illustrated on the direction page and write a story about the adventures of the person wearing this glove.

MATERIALS NEEDED

pictures of gloves on page 33
pencils or pens
writing paper
colored construction paper
scissors
glue

HANG YOUR FINISHED GLOVE STORIES ON THE CLOTHESLINE.

THE GLOVE CENTER

DIRECTIONS FOR THE GLOVE CENTER

GLUE

PENCILS

DIRECTIONS FOR
THE GLOVE CENTER

1. Pick *one* pair of gloves pictured below.

2. Who is wearing this pair of gloves? Write a short story about an adventure the person has while wearing the gloves you selected.

3. Draw a large picture of the glove you selected. Mount your story inside the glove.

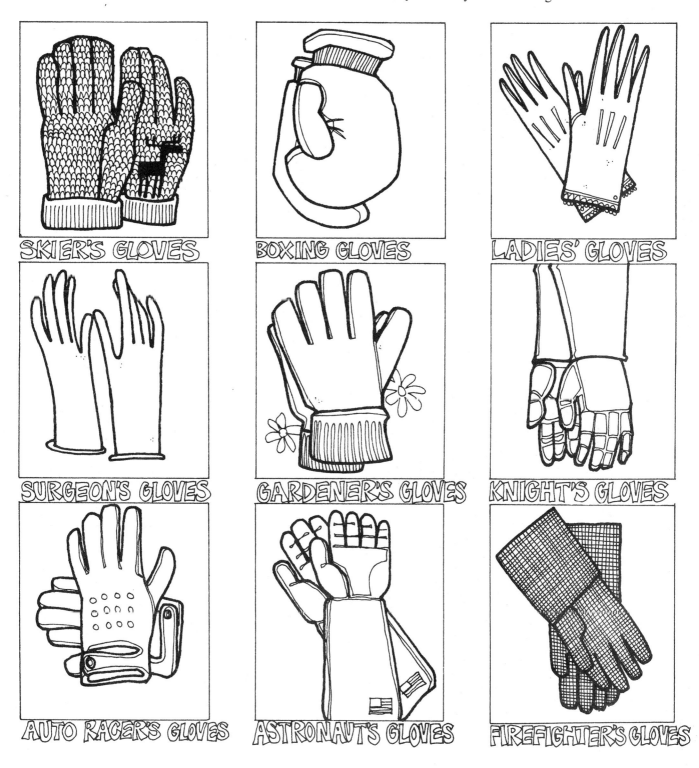

SKIER'S GLOVES BOXING GLOVES LADIES' GLOVES

SURGEON'S GLOVES GARDENER'S GLOVES KNIGHT'S GLOVES

AUTO RACER'S GLOVES ASTRONAUT'S GLOVES FIREFIGHTER'S GLOVES

BOOK PAL CENTER

A CENTER SUMMARY

Each student is assigned a child in the first grade to be a book pal. Original stories are written and illustrated for the book pal. The completed book is presented to the first grader as a present.

MATERIALS NEEDED

list of first graders
scratch paper
pencils
magic markers
white art paper for final copy of book
colored paper for cover
heavy tape (for binding)
list of interview questions
stapler

BOOK PAL CENTER

DIRECTIONS FOR BOOK PAL CENTER

INTERVIEW QUESTIONS
1. _____
2. _____
3. _____
4. _____

BOOK PALS

AMY · JASON
BRAD · BILLY
CARLOS · JULIE
DICK · ANDY
ELLEN · LAURA
FRED · MARK

GARY · LINDA
HANK · MICHAEL
JAN · BRIAN
KAREN · MONICA
LISA · STEVEN
MATT · ROGER

NANCY · CHRIS
PAT · TAMI
RITA · CLAUDIA
SALLY · ALAN
TIM · ELIZABETH
WALTER · PAUL

← LOOK AT THESE BOOKS FOR IDEAS.

PENCILS

FELT PENS

WHERE THE WILD THINGS ARE
GREEN EGGS AND HAM
Animals on the Farm
THE THREE BEARS
Winnie-the-Pooh
MY ABC BOOK
The Little House
PINOCCHIO
MOTHER GOOSE
THE BIG BOOK OF TRUCKS
Hansel and Gretel
RIDDLES
Hop on Pop

PAPER DRAWER

TAPE, GLUE, TACKS, PASTE, & STAPLERS

SUGGESTED QUESTIONS TO ASK BOOK PAL

1. How old are you?

2. Do you have any brothers or sisters? What are their names?

3. Who are your best friends?

4. Do you have a pet? What kind? What is your pet's name?

5. What is your favorite color?

6. What kind of book would you like me to write for you?

    animal _____   circus _____   fairy tale _____   mystery _____   adventure _____

CENTER SOLUTION

1. You will be assigned a "book pal" from the first grade. Write a book for your boy or girl.

2. On "Interview Day" meet and talk with your "book pal" so you will have a better idea of what your "book pal" likes.

3. Write a story for your "book pal" using scratch paper.

4. When your story is checked for spelling mistakes, copy the story on white art paper. Write only one or two sentences on each page. Print in large, clear letters.

5. Illustrate each page using magic markers.

6. Decorate a cover for your book, using colored paper. Add a title page with your name as author and illustrator. You might want to include a dedication page in your book such as:

   THIS BOOK WAS WRITTEN ESPECIALLY FOR MY BOOK PAL
   RANDY SMITH
   OF ROOM 6

7. Staple your book and bind it with tape. Present your book to your "book pal" as a present after reading your story to her/him.

MAGAZINE POSTER CENTER

A CENTER SUMMARY

After writing poems, students cut letters from magazine ads, headlines, and articles for each word of their poem instead of writing the poems with pencils. The letters are mounted on colored paper and displayed as posters.

MATERIALS NEEDED

colored paper
scissors
glue
magazines
pencil
scratch paper (for rough draft of poem)

SUGGESTED TOPICS FOR POEMS

Friendship
My Pet
Yellow (or any color)
Freedom
Feelings
Sisters (brothers)
Trees

DIRECTIONS FOR
MAGAZINE POSTER CENTER

1. Using the scratch paper at the center, write a poem. Use the suggested topics or select one of your own. Your poem does not have to rhyme.

2. When your poem is finished, find the letters you need for each word by going through the magazines at the center. Sometimes you will find your entire word in an ad or article. Sometimes you will have to cut letters from several different ads to spell the word you need.

3. Place your cut-out letters and words on colored paper. Arrange them so they fit properly and are spaced well.

4. Glue the cut-out letters to the colored paper. Give your poem a title.

Yellow: the COLOR of lemons & sun, OF butter on A CINNAMON BUN, the color of lollipops & SAND, of CHICKS and the pencil IN my HAND.

YELLOW

CREATE A COMMERCIAL CENTER

A CENTER SUMMARY

Students create an original product and write a commercial appropriate for television.
Students design a container for their product and make up their own slogans or jingles.
Have Commercial Day in your classroom, when students present their ads to the class.
Award prizes for the most creative ads and package designs.

MATERIALS NEEDED

writing paper
pencils or pens
empty cartons, cans, boxes, etc.
colored paper
magic markers, crayons
scissors
glue

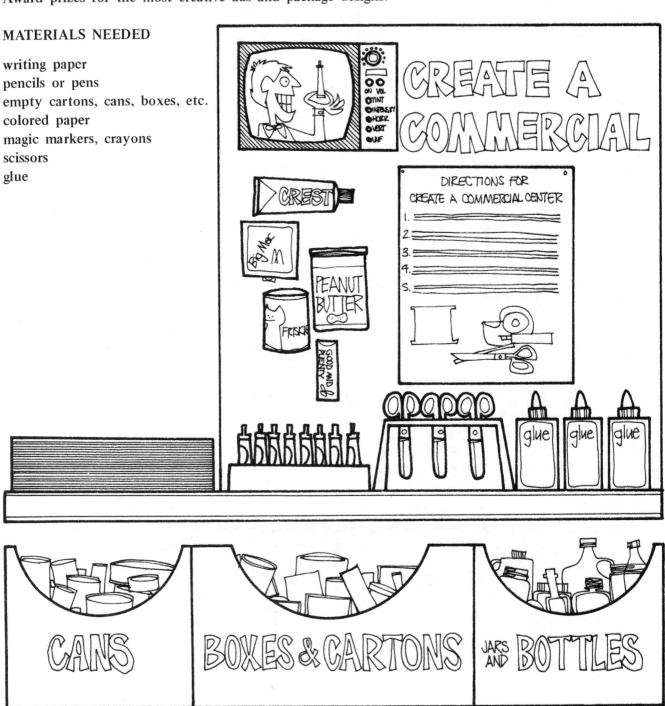

MORE IDEAS . . .

If your school has videotape equipment, have students film their commercials.

DIRECTIONS FOR
CREATE A COMMERCIAL CENTER

1. Select a product that you plan to introduce on television for the first time. It may be a new cereal, soup, soap, toy, or whatever you wish.

2. Pick a name for your product – one that is original and matches the type of product you are selling. Examples: Toothpaste – "Refresh," Vitamin – "Pep."

3. Write a commercial that would be suitable for television. Make up a slogan or jingle to help sell your product.

4. Be sure to include the following information about your product:
   a. what it is
   b. why it is different from other products on the market
   c. why people *need* your product
   d. where people can buy it

5. Now have fun designing a container for your product. Bring in an empty carton, tube, box, can, or any suitable container for your product. Decorate the container, making it colorful and appealing. Include important information on the box, such as ingredients, nutrients, your slogan, or whatever applies to your product.

6. Present your commercial to the class. Try to "sell" your product to them.

THE CREST CENTER

A CENTER SUMMARY

Students design a family crest and answer six questions about themselves using only pictures in the six sections of the shield.

MATERIALS NEEDED

white drawing paper
pencils (for rough draft)
magic markers
reference books showing crests and coats-of-arms (optional)
scissors

DIRECTIONS FOR
THE CREST CENTER

1. Draw a large crest on a piece of white drawing paper. Copy a crest below or design one of your own. Divide your crest into six sections as shown.

2. Answer each of the following questions in a section of your crest. Use pictures only; *no words are allowed.* Color each picture.

   a. Who are the people in your family?
   b. What are two things you enjoy doing with your family?
   c. What are three things you are good at?
   d. What are two things you would like to improve about yourself?
   e. What are your favorite hobbies or interests?
   f. What occupation would you like to have in the future?

3. Cut out your crest when you are finished.

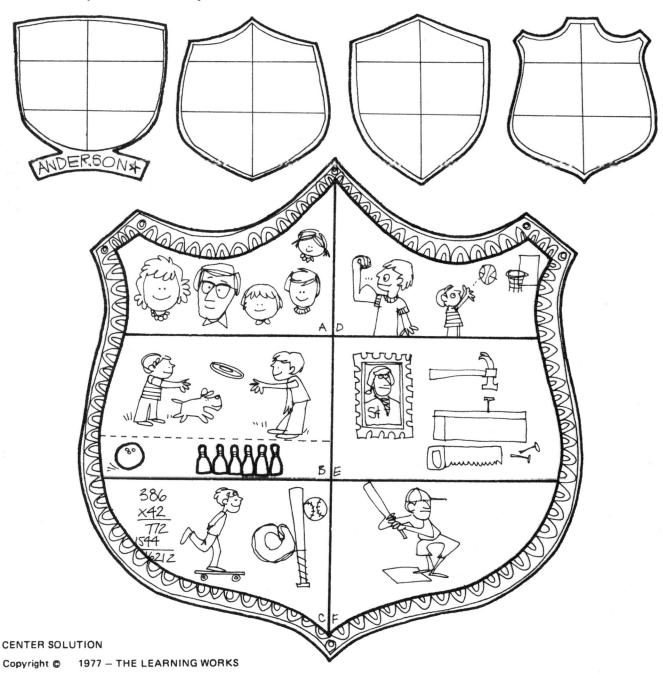

THE THING CENTER

A CENTER SUMMARY

Students use their imagination to create a "thing" which can be anything they want it to be. Students write about their thing, draw their thing and can even write a song or poem about the thing.

MATERIALS NEEDED

writing paper
pencils
magic markers

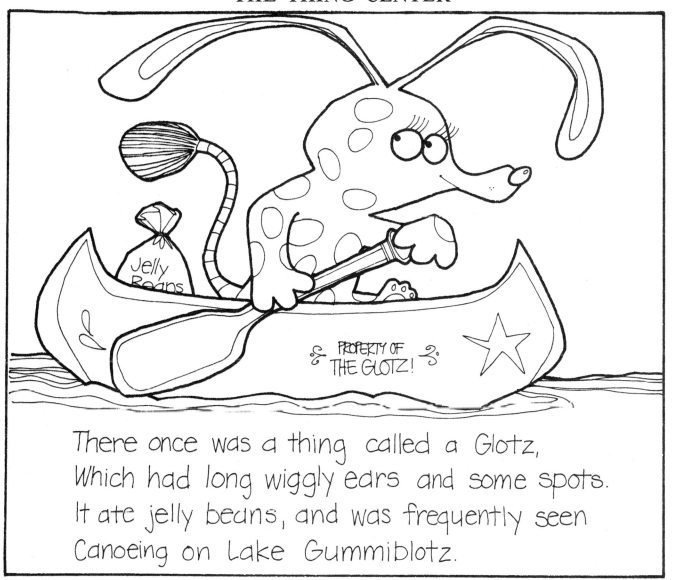

There once was a thing called a Glotz,
Which had long wiggly ears and some spots.
It ate jelly beans, and was frequently seen
Canoeing on Lake Gummiblotz.

YOU HAVE JUST SEEN THE "THING"!

Write a paragraph describing the THING. Be sure to use colorful words. Tell what the THING looks like, where the THING can be found, what noises the THING makes, how to take care of the THING, the THING's likes and dislikes, and unusual features of the THING;

OR . . .

write a song about the THING – a ballad, a rock song, a lullaby or any kind of song;

OR . . .

write a short story starring the THING;

OR . . .

write a poem about the THING. The poem can be free verse, a limerick, haiku – whatever you wish.

CENTER SOLUTION

MAKE-A-WORD CENTER

A CENTER SUMMARY

Students select two words from the make-a-word chart and create a make-believe object.
Students illustrate and write a short story about their objects.

MATERIALS NEEDED

crayons or magic markers
pencils
writing paper
colored paper
glue

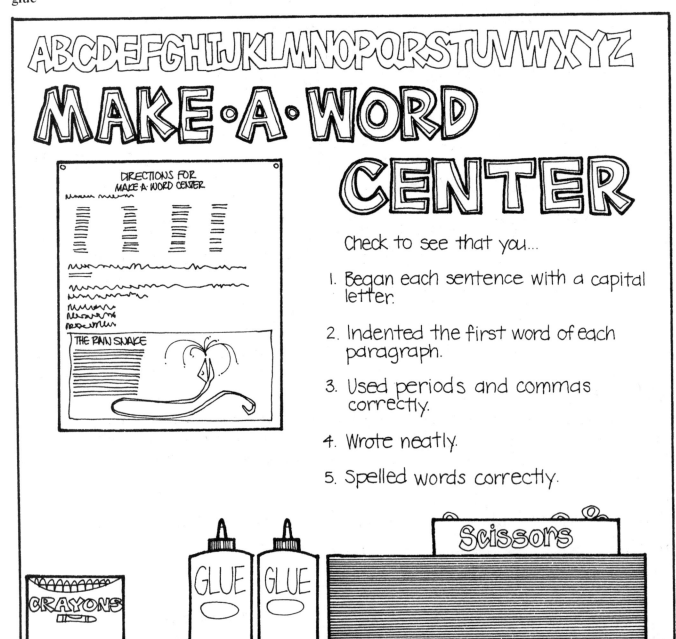

ABCDEFGHIJKLMNOPQRSTUVWXYZ

MAKE·A·WORD CENTER

DIRECTIONS FOR MAKE·A·WORD CENTER

THE RAIN SNAKE

Check to see that you...

1. Began each sentence with a capital letter.

2. Indented the first word of each paragraph.

3. Used periods and commas correctly.

4. Wrote neatly.

5. Spelled words correctly.

CRAYONS

GLUE GLUE

Scissors

1. Look at the following list of words:

BOAT	RAIN	PIZZA	TELEPHONE
OWL	MUSIC	FROG	WAND
POTATO	SNAKE	TREE	TRUCK
BEE	MELON	QUEEN	PIE
FUDGE	FLOWER	PEACH	SCHOOL
PENCIL	CLOCK	CANDY	NOSE

2. Pick any two words to put together. Create a make-believe word.
   Example: A MELON BEE

3. Draw a picture of your two words on a piece of drawing paper. Write your new word at the top of your paper.

4. Write a short story about your new word.
   a. What does it look like?
   b. Where can it be found?
   c. What can it do?

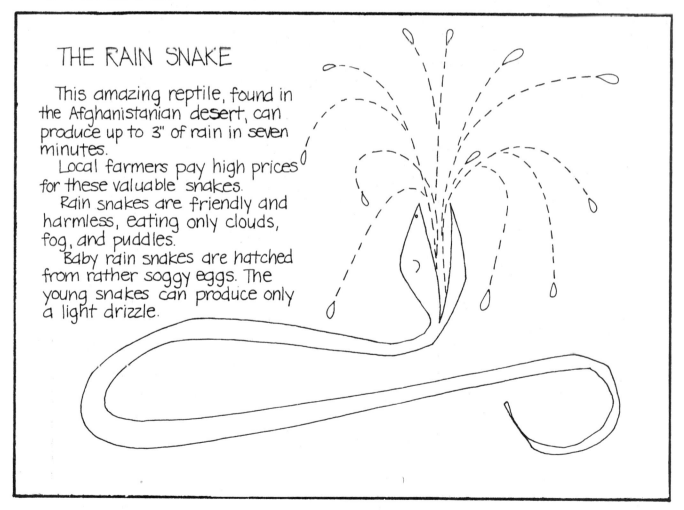

THE RAIN SNAKE

This amazing reptile, found in the Afghanistanian desert, can produce up to 3" of rain in seven minutes.

Local farmers pay high prices for these valuable snakes.

Rain snakes are friendly and harmless, eating only clouds, fog, and puddles.

Baby rain snakes are hatched from rather soggy eggs. The young snakes can produce only a light drizzle.

ON THE SCENE CENTER

A CENTER SUMMARY

Students write a descriptive paragraph including use of each of the senses: sight, touch, taste, smell, and sound.

MATERIALS NEEDED

writing paper
pencil or pen

CENTER SOLUTION

DIRECTIONS FOR
ON THE SCENE CENTER

1. Pick one of the locations listed below or choose your own setting to write about.

2. In your description of this setting, use each of the five senses and describe:

    a. what it looks like

    b. what it sounds like

    c. what it feels like

    d. what it smells like

    e. what it tastes like

3. Close your eyes and try to imagine you are actually there. Write vividly and capture a definite mood of your scene. Can you make it seem real to another person?

4. Here are some suggestions for locations to write about:

    an empty stadium

    a beach at sunset

    in the middle of a traffic jam on the freeway

    caught in a rainstorm walking home from school

    sitting in the dentist's office waiting for your turn

    under the circus big top

    alone in a meadow

    in your favorite bakery

    in a department store during a sale

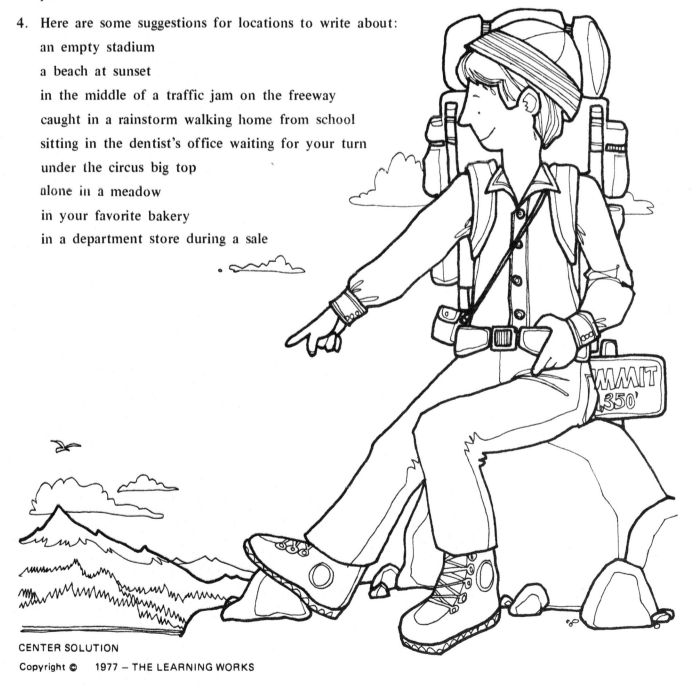

BEHIND THE DOOR CENTER

A CENTER SUMMARY

Students create a door using colored construction paper. Students then use the door as an "idea starter" for a creative writing story.

MATERIALS NEEDED

colored paper (for the door)
scissors
writing paper for the story
pencil or pen
glue

CENTER SOLUTION

DIRECTIONS FOR
BEHIND THE DOOR CENTER

1. Think of different types of doors, such as:
   a doctor's door
   a castle door
   the door of a submarine
   a rocket ship's door
   a prison door
   a hotel's door

2. Pick a door from the list or make up one of your own. Draw your door on construction paper.

3. Cut your door out.

4. Pretend you are actually going through your door and tell about your adventures. Write a short story about what takes place BEHIND THE DOOR.

5. Display your door and story for others to share.

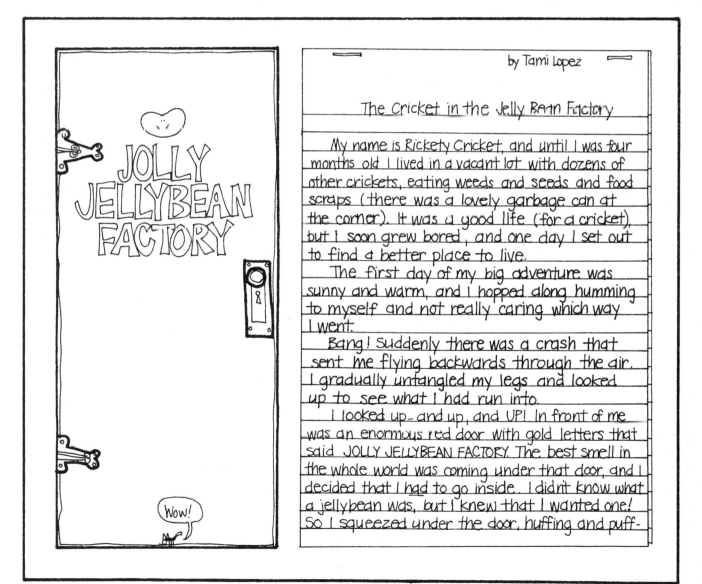

by Tami Lopez

The Cricket in the Jelly Bean Factory

My name is Rickety Cricket, and until I was four months old I lived in a vacant lot with dozens of other crickets, eating weeds and seeds and food scraps (there was a lovely garbage can at the corner). It was a good life (for a cricket), but I soon grew bored, and one day I set out to find a better place to live.

The first day of my big adventure was sunny and warm, and I hopped along humming to myself and not really caring which way I went.

Bang! Suddenly there was a crash that sent me flying backwards through the air. I gradually untangled my legs and looked up to see what I had run into.

I looked up - and up, and UP! In front of me was an enormous red door with gold letters that said JOLLY JELLYBEAN FACTORY. The best smell in the whole world was coming under that door, and I decided that I had to go inside. I didn't know what a jellybean was, but I knew that I wanted one! So I squeezed under the door, huffing and puff-

Wow!

CENTER SOLUTION

NOTES

DICTIONARY SKILLS CENTERS

ALPHABETICAL SPORTS

A CENTER SUMMARY

Students list various sports in alphabetical order as they would appear in the dictionary.

MATERIALS NEEDED

ditto of Alphabetical Sports
pencils or pens

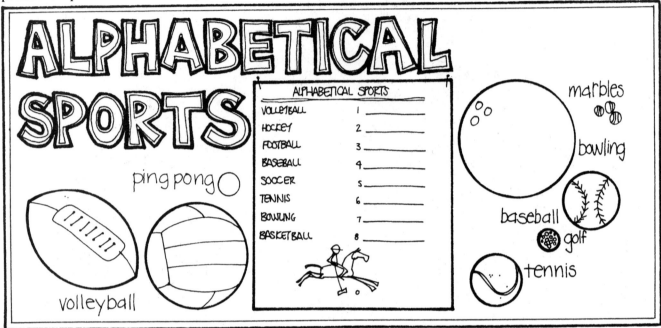

ANSWERS TO ALPHABETICAL SPORTS

1. badminton
2. baseball
3. basketball
4. bowling
5. fencing
6. football
7. golf
8. handball
9. hockey
10. judo
11. ping-pong
12. polo
13. skiing
14. soccer
15. tennis
16. volleyball

MORE IDEAS . . .

Have students write the following games in alphabetical order.

jacks
cards
marbles
bingo
chess
checkers
tag
catch

CENTER SOLUTION

ALPHABETICAL SPORTS

Words are listed in alphabetical order in the dictionary. Write these sports in alphabetical order as they would appear in the dictionary.

VOLLEYBALL	1. _____
HOCKEY	2. _____
FOOTBALL	3. _____
BASEBALL	4. _____
SOCCER	5. _____
TENNIS	6. _____
BOWLING	7. _____
BASKETBALL	8. _____
FENCING	9. _____
BADMINTON	10. _____
PING-PONG	11. _____
JUDO	12. _____
POLO	13. _____
HANDBALL	14. _____
SKIING	15. _____
GOLF	16. _____

GUIDE WORD SAFARI

A CENTER SUMMARY

A hypothetical dictionary page is given with two guide words. Students must decide which word would not belong on the page.

MATERIALS NEEDED

ditto of Guide Word Safari
pencils or pens
dictionary

ANSWERS TO GUIDE WORD SAFARI

1. despise
2. mental
3. blood
4. invoke
5. voter
6. home
7. refuse
8. contend

"goose" and "gorilla" have "gopher" between them on the GUIDE WORD SAFARI

MORE IDEAS . . .

Have students use the dictionary and write the guide words for each of the following:

1. staff _____ _____

2. picnic _____ _____

3. medicine _____ _____

4. reach _____ _____

5. down _____ _____

CENTER SOLUTION

GUIDE WORD SAFARI

In each exercise below, two guide words are given followed by four words. Write the one word that would NOT be found on the dictionary page containing each set of guide words.

EXAMPLE: ABSURD   ACCEPT

abuse
accede
accent
access

1. DESCRIPTION   DESPERATE

desire
despair
despise
desk

2. MERE   MESS

merit
meson
mesa
mental

3. BLAZE   BLISTER

blimp
bleach
blood
bless

4. INWARD   IRON

iris
invoke
ion
irk

5. VOLCANIC   VOTE

vote
vortex
volley
voter

6. HOBO   HOLDER

home
hold
hockey
hogan

7. REGIMENT   REGULAR

regret
register
refuse
region

8. CONSTRICT   CONTEMPT

contemplate
construct
contain
contend

PROPER PRONUNCIATION

A CENTER SUMMARY

Students use a dictionary to find the proper pronunciation of given words. After writing the phonetic spelling they mark the rhyming word.

MATERIALS NEEDED

ditto of Proper Pronunciation
pencils or pens
dictionary

ANSWERS TO PROPER PRONUNCIATION

1. (shēf) — leaf
2. (rō) — slow
3. (prī·ər) — fryer
4. (mō·tēf) — relief
5. (jĭngks) — sinks
6. (sĭv) — give

7. (jĭb) — crib
8. (kŏ·kĕt) — regret
9. (fān) — rain
10. (brīne) — dine
11. (pīd) — hide
12. (krō·shā) — relay

MORE IDEAS . . .

Here are the phonetic spellings of five popular animals. Have students write the name of each animal.

1. jə·răf
2. lī·ən
3. mŭng·kē
4. ĕl·ə·fent
5. ăn·tə·lōp

CENTER SOLUTION

PROPER PRONUNCIATION

Look up each word below in the dictionary. Write the correct pronunciation (or phonetic spelling) on the line. Underline the word that rhymes.

Example: CARE _____kâr_____   far or <u>hair</u>

1. SHEAF   _____   leaf or chef

2. ROE   _____   shoe or slow

3. PRIOR   _____   freer or fryer

4. MOTIF   _____   relief or whiff

5. JINX   _____   fix or sinks

6. SIEVE   _____   give or receive

7. JIB   _____   describe or crib

8. COQUETTE _____   banquet or regret

9. FEIGN   _____   rain or sign

10. BRINE   _____   seen or dine

11. PIED   _____   feed or hide

12. CROCHET _____   hatchet or relay

THE PIED PIPER

MIXED MEANINGS

A CENTER SUMMARY

Students use the dictionary to discover that many words have more than one meaning. Students match definitions as they are used in the context of sentences.

MATERIALS NEEDED

ditto of Mixed Meanings
pencils or pens

ANSWERS TO MIXED MEANINGS

CUT	a. 2	b. 4	c. 1	d. 3
POINT	a. 1	b. 3	c. 2	d. 4
SLIDE	a. 4	b. 2	c. 3	d. 1

MIXED MEANINGS

Many words have more than one definition. Four meanings are given for each word below. Match the correct definition as it is used in each sentence.

CUT

1. to reduce or make less
2. to eliminate or remove
3. to go through, cross
4. to divide or separate as with a sharp tool

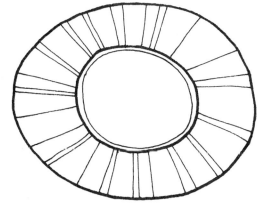

a. We had to <u>cut</u> her part out of the play. _____

b. Mother <u>cut</u> out the dress pattern. _____

c. During the sale, the price of milk was <u>cut</u>. _____

d. The new highway will not <u>cut</u> through the center of town. _____

POINT

1. tip
2. object or purpose
3. detail
4. certain stage in a process

THE OTTER BUILDS A MUD <u>SLIDE</u> TO PLAY ON.

a. I just broke the <u>point</u> of my pencil. _____

b. Underline each main <u>point</u> you want to stress in your report. _____

c. There is no <u>point</u> in continuing this discussion. _____

d. When the candy reaches the boiling <u>point</u>, then you must adjust the heat. _____

SLIDE

1. smooth surface on which a person or thing may move
2. avalanche
3. piece of glass on which one can examine objects under a microscope
4. a picture projected on a screen

a. The <u>slide</u> of our vacation is my favorite. _____

b. That rock <u>slide</u> just missed our car! _____

c. The doctor prepared the <u>slide</u> for a closer examination of the bacteria. _____

d. The children love to go on the <u>slide</u>. _____

WORLD-WIDE WORDS

A CENTER SUMMARY

Students use the dictionary definitions to match words with the place each is associated with.

MATERIALS NEEDED

ditto of World-Wide Words
dictionaries
pencils or pens

ANSWERS TO WORLD-WIDE WORDS

1. H
2. C
3. I
4. E
5. J
6. D
7. A
8. F
9. B
10. G
11. D
12. F

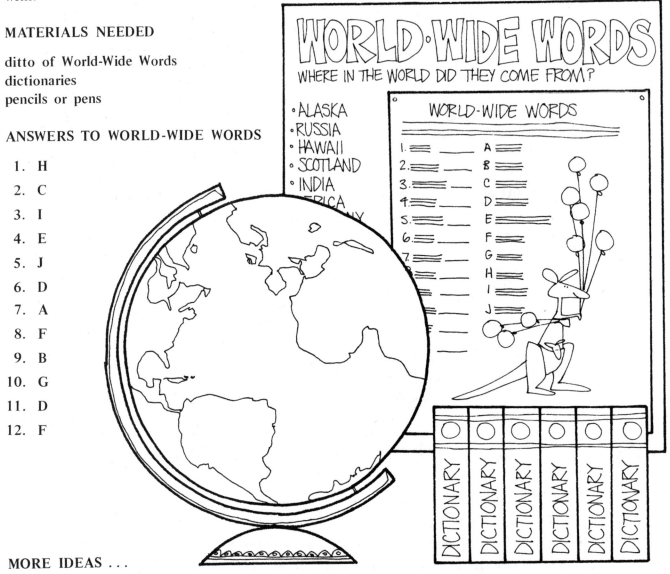

MORE IDEAS . . .

Have students match these definitions with word list A from World-Wide Words.

a. a boat
b. a metal urn
c. a parakeet
d. a young child
e. a weapon
f. money

g. a long garment
h. a restaurant
i. a cap
j. a tree
k. a food
l. an animal related to the giraffe

ANSWERS

1. e   2. k   3. c   4. g   5. f   6. i   7. a   8. j   9. b   10. h   11. d   12. l

CENTER SOLUTION

WORLD-WIDE WORDS

DIRECTIONS: For each word, match the place where it can be located. Some answers are used twice. Use your dictionary for help.

<u>A</u>

1. bola _____
2. poi _____
3. budgerigar _____
4. sari _____
5. balboa _____
6. tam-o'-shanter _____
7. umiak _____
8. baobab _____
9. samovar _____
10. rathskeller _____
11. bairn _____
12. okapi _____

<u>B</u>

A. Alaska
B. Russia
C. Hawaii
D. Scotland
E. India or Pakistan
F. Africa
G. Germany
H. South America
I. Australia
J. Panama

PICTURE PUZZLERS

A CENTER SUMMARY

Students use dictionary definitions to match a word to a given picture.

MATERIALS NEEDED

ditto of Picture Puzzlers
dictionaries
pencils or pens

ANSWERS TO PICTURE PUZZLERS

1. C	7. D
2. F	8. J
3. B	9. H
4. G	10. K
5. E	11. L
6. I	12. A

MORE IDEAS ...

Have students use the dictionary and draw pictures for the following words:

1. epaulet
2. maracas
3. talon
4. fez
5. akimbo

OR ...

Have students find words in the dictionary and create their own Picture Puzzlers for others in the class to solve.

CENTER SOLUTION

PICTURE PUZZLERS

DIRECTIONS: Match the following words to the pictures. (Use your dictionary for help.) Write the correct letter on the line by each word.

1. _____ chaps
2. _____ gibbon
3. _____ cornucopia
4. _____ puffin
5. _____ caravel
6. _____ ascot

7. _____ marimba
8. _____ sconce
9. _____ gladiolus
10. _____ coronet
11. _____ queue
12. _____ hod

CENTER SOLUTION

Copyright © 1977 – THE LEARNING WORKS

SLANG TIME

A CENTER SUMMARY

Students use the dictionary to look up slang definitions and then match the slang to the proper meaning.

MATERIALS NEEDED

ditto of Slang Time
pencils or pens
dictionaries

ANSWERS TO SLANG TIME

1.	F	7.	A
2.	K	8.	I
3.	H	9.	J
4.	C	10.	D
5.	E	11.	L
6.	G	12.	B

SLANG TIME

Slang is an informal, nonstandard manner of speaking. Match the following slang words or expressions with their meanings. Use your dictionary for help.

ANSWERS

_____ 1. nifty	A.	business
_____ 2. bunk	B.	foolishly sentimental
_____ 3. string bean	C.	to run away
_____ 4. vamoose	D.	an expert
_____ 5. grand	E.	a thousand dollars
_____ 6. jump	F.	excellent
_____ 7. game	G.	to get an advantage over
_____ 8. hot	H.	very tall
_____ 9. burn up	I.	stolen
_____ 10. hot shot	J.	to make angry or enraged
_____ 11. clobber	K.	empty talk, lies, nonsense
_____ 12. corny	L.	to beat or pound severely

VAMOOSE, MOOSE!

DICTIONARY DEMONS

A CENTER SUMMARY

Students use their dictionary to look up definitions and answer questions about words.

MATERIALS NEEDED

ditto of Dictionary Demons
dictionaries
pencils or pens

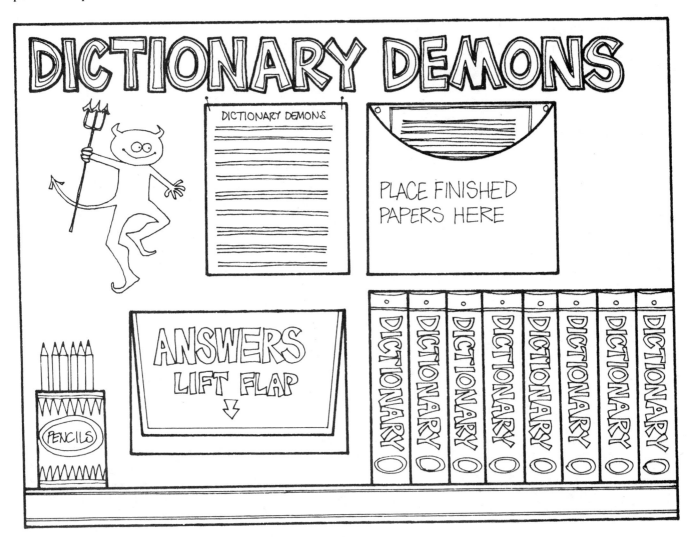

ANSWERS TO DICTIONARY DEMONS

1. clumsy, stupid person
2. orange
3. arrows
4. sword
5. eat it
6. reddish-purple

7. a tree
8. disinfectant
9. birds
10. resentment
11. noisy
12. aster

CENTER SOLUTION

DICTIONARY DEMONS

DIRECTIONS: Look up each underlined word in the dictionary. Answer each question below.

1. What is a lummox? ——————————————————

2. What color is a persimmon? ——————————————

3. What would you put in a quiver? ——————————————

4. What is another name for a cutlass? ——————————

5. What would you most likely do with rutabaga? ——————

6. If you had a magenta dress, what color would it be? ——————

7. What is a kari? ——————————————————

8. What is cresol used for? ——————————————

9. Ornithology deals with the study of what animal? ——————

10. What is another word for umbrage? ——————————

11. A vociferous audience would be what kind of audience? ————

12. The arnica is related to what plant? ——————————

persimmon

WHO'S WHO?

A CENTER SUMMARY

Students use the dictionary to find the definitions for given words and then classify them into one of two groups – mammal or bird.

MATERIALS NEEDED

ditto of Who's Who?
dictionaries
pencils or pens

ANSWERS FOR WHO'S WHO?

1. M
2. M
3. B
4. M
5. B
6. B
7. M
8. M
9. B
10. M
11. B
12. B
13. M
14. B
15. M
16. B
17. B
18. B
19. M
20. M

MORE IDEAS . . .

Write the following names on the board. Have students use the dictionary to find and circle the names of six plants or flowers from this list:

1. phlox
2. saguaro
3. jerkin
4. sorghum
5. jerboa
6. rhododendron
7. carp
8. trident
9. aphid
10. aster
11. cutlass
12. yew
13. dollop
14. langur
15. camisole

ANSWERS

1, 2, 4, 6, 10, 12

CENTER SOLUTION

WHO'S WHO?

Listed below are the names of mammals and birds. Look up each word in the dictionary. Write M (mammal) or B (bird) for each word.

1. dobbin _____
2. vole _____
3. quetzal _____
4. wombat _____
5. osprey _____
6. plover _____
7. zebu _____
8. eland _____
9. puffin _____
10. tapir _____

11. ptarmigan _____
12. kiwi _____
13. shrew _____
14. rook _____
15. wolverine _____
16. snipe _____
17. jackdaw _____
18. rhea _____
19. koala _____
20. yak _____

ani

agama

agouti

axolotl

apus

addax

antpitta

amphisbaena

angwantibo

DAFFY DICTIONARY CENTER

A CENTER SUMMARY

At this center, students make up an original word, illustrate their word, name the part of speech, and then define the word.

MATERIALS NEEDED

drawing paper
a dictionary (to make sure students' words are original)
colored pencils
magic markers

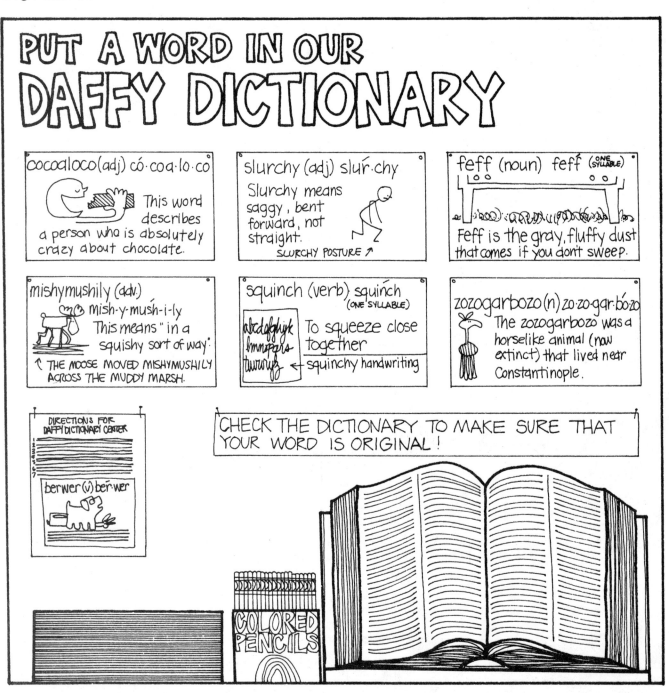

CENTER SOLUTION

DIRECTIONS FOR
DAFFY DICTIONARY CENTER

1. Make up a word you have never heard before.

2. Look up your word in the dictionary at the center. If you find it there, make up a new word. Your word must be original.

3. Write your new word in large letters across the top of your paper.

4. Write the correct part of speech for your word. Is your word a noun (n.)? Verb (v.)? Adjective (adj.)? Adverb (adv.)?

5. Divide your word into syllables and mark the accent or stress mark so other students will know how to pronounce your word.

6. Draw a picture of your word to *show* others what it means.

7. Define or tell what your word means in one or two sentences.

TWISTED SAYINGS CENTER

A CENTER SUMMARY

Students take a famous saying or proverb and change words so it says the same thing but sounds very different. This is an excellent way to introduce the use of a dictionary and thesaurus.

MATERIALS NEEDED

a dictionary
a thesaurus
pencils or pens
white drawing paper
crayons, magic markers, colored pencils

EXAMPLE: A cooking receptacle kept under close surveillance will not attain a temperature of 100°c.

CENTER SOLUTION

DIRECTIONS FOR
TWISTED SAYINGS CENTER

1. Pick a famous saying or proverb from the list below.

2. Change as many words as you can so it means the same thing but sounds very different. Use the thesaurus to help you.

3. Write your final saying on white drawing paper, illustrate it, and then color it with crayons, magic markers or colored pencils.

It is virtually impossible to instruct an aging canine in the art of performing novel antics. (In other words, you can't teach an old dog new tricks!)

Famous sayings and proverbs:

A PENNY FOR YOUR THOUGHTS

DON'T GIVE UP THE SHIP

AN APPLE A DAY KEEPS THE DOCTOR AWAY

GIVE ME LIBERTY OR GIVE ME DEATH

DON'T CRY OVER SPILLED MILK

TOO MANY COOKS SPOIL THE BROTH

THE ONLY THING WE HAVE TO FEAR IS FEAR ITSELF

THERE IS NO SUBSTITUTE FOR HARD WORK

SPEAK SOFTLY AND CARRY A BIG STICK

DON'T FIRE UNTIL YOU SEE THE WHITES OF THEIR EYES

I REGRET THAT I HAVE BUT ONE LIFE TO LOSE FOR MY COUNTRY

ASK NOT WHAT YOUR COUNTRY CAN DO FOR YOU; ASK WHAT YOU CAN DO FOR YOUR COUNTRY

A BIRD IN THE HAND IS WORTH TWO IN THE BUSH

A ROLLING STONE GATHERS NO MOSS

A STITCH IN TIME SAVES NINE

CENTER SOLUTION

NOTES